This book is being given to

_____

because we care about your leadership growth.

_____

Praise for *Execute to Win*

"Execute to Win challenges high performers to leave an extraordinary legacy by setting worthy goals and focusing on becoming better each and every day."
—Ben Newman, best-selling author of *Leave YOUR Legacy*

"Driven leaders want to win—plain and simple. Execute to Win *provides a framework that helps to inform and guide today's driven leaders toward the success that they desire for themselves and the teams they lead. It's all about execution, and this book will provide the reader with salient insights as to what it really takes to drive winning results."*
—Dave Charest, President and CEO, Atrilogy Solutions Group

"Execute to Win *is a great tool for leading executives who want to achieve meaningful goals, delegate more effectively, and improve productivity in less time."*
—Dena Ladd, Executive Director, Missouri Cures

"Vidal and Finkelstein provide a practical tool kit for maintaining organizational focus and driving bottom-line results. Execute to Win *is an insightful recipe for consistently achieving success based on people-centric leadership practices that maximize culture, transparency, focus, and team-based execution across the organization. Execute to Win *is about winning through focused execution, all the time."*
—Douglas S. Archibald, Senior Vice President, Information Builders

"Execute to Win *is a book that finely and strategically presents the concepts of a winning culture and business success through team building and coaching. What I like particularly in this book is how the authors lay out the 'how' in leading work teams to strengthened cohesion and achievement as well as presenting a tactical road map of best practices, exploring competencies and skill enrichment. I recommend this book for those that desire to be successful leaders in their companies because it teaches 'winning leadership' for executives and business owners in the way to build and win like professional sports coaches, general managers, and owners."*

—Dr. Leroy Simpson, industrial and organizational psychologist

"Steve and René have written a must-read primer for leaders who want to win by achieving desired results. Execute to Win *is an articulate, comprehensive, and focused framework that will prepare any person who aspires to become a better leader."*

—Eric X. Hernandez, Senior Director PMO,
Amcor Rigid Plastics

"Execution is the crux of business. In Execute to Win, *René and Steve distill the solution to complex business problems into a simple set of practical instructions that make execution easy and fun!"*

—Eric Humes, CEO, Keystone Technologies

"Execute to Win: How Leaders Get Results is the road map to maximize your influence and accomplishments. Whether in business or life, selling a product or service, or persuading a team or individual, mastering the skills identified will prepare you to accomplish more than you ever imagined."*

—Frank V. Danzo, author of People Hire People, Not Resumes

"Execute to Win: How Leaders Get Results is a must-read for those who recognize the importance of execution and want to go deeper. By describing the linkages among behaviors, execution, and results, René and Steve have illuminated many of the most important points of leverage for improved performance."*

—Glen Justis, Founder and CEO, Acclaim Strategies, LLC

"Execute to Win *is a great read offering practical checklists that help keep leaders on track to achieve results."*

—Helen Jardine, Chief Development Officer, Northwestern Mutual

"A great playbook for leaders and teams who want to grow and optimize their potential."

—Irl Scissors, Founding Principal, Gateway Government Relations

"In my years as an international consultant, I've found that many organizations, both here in the States and overseas, have team members with wonderful ideas and strategies but lacked the simple fundamentals of knowing how to execute them. Execute to Win *offers a pragmatic approach to helping leaders and teams execute their ideas and accomplish their goals. A must-read to help any organization progress."*

—James H. Canada, author, speaker, international consultant, and CEO of Alliance Technologies / Business Solutions

"With Execute to Win, *Vidal and Finkelstein deliver proof of concept. They have executed a winning how-to for those who are past the desire for pithy platitudes and are ready to commit to the attitudes and behaviors that define the road to true success."*

—Kent Reynolds, Financial Wealth Advisor, J.P. Morgan

"René and Steve have nailed it with their latest book, Execute to Win. *Using their experience as coaches of high-performing athletes and business leaders, René and Steve outline in this book the ten essential skills of execution and then help the reader take a deep dive into each of those skills. It is not just the* what *that they explain so succinctly, it is the 'Now what?' If you want to 'win' more in life and business,* Execute to Win *is a must-read."*

—Lisa Nichols, CEO, Technology Partners

Execute to Win

HOW LEADERS GET RESULTS

René Vidal and Steve Finkelstein

Also by René Vidal and Steve Finkelstein

Play Smart to Win in Business
Leadership Lessons from Center Court to Corner Office

Contents

INTRODUCTION

Create a Culture of Execution

*The greatest gap in the world is the one
between knowing and doing.*
—JON GORDON, AUTHOR OF *TRAINING CAMP*

The number-one stumbling block for leaders, teams, and organizations is ineffective execution. It's not lack of knowledge, ideas, or strategies. In fact, strategies most often fail because they aren't executed well. Execution is what happens between aspirations and results.

The "execution gap" is the difference between knowing and doing, and that's exactly what this book is about. *Execute to Win* is a tool leaders can use to help others consistently perform at the highest level.

As a leader, what percentage of your projects are done on time and on budget and achieve the stated benefits?

Just imagine what your results would be if you could improve project execution, sales success, performance, and productivity by 10 percent, 20 percent, or even 50 percent!

Great leaders create cultures of excellence in execution, operating from the premise that execution is the job of everyone.

Sports and Business

Our lives have centered on helping leaders and teams win. René is a successful head coach, six-time NCAA tennis champion, and nationally-recognized speaker on winning leadership. Steve is an expert in business execution and cofounder of Experience on Demand, which was voted the number-one management consulting firm in St. Louis by *Small Business Monthly* readers (2013, 2014, 2016, 2017, and 2019).

Whether it's sports or business, what we've learned is this: winning and losing doesn't come down to trick plays, game science, or new systems.

What drives results is execution.

We've combined fifty-plus years of extensive work with top athletes, teams, universities, businesses, nonprofits, and larger organizations and over two hundred leadership conversations with CEOs, business leaders, Olympic champions, best-selling authors, and successful entrepreneurs to distill what it takes to achieve excellence in execution.

As a result, we discovered ten distinct skills that drive winning execution.

#1: Leadership

Leadership is the ability to get results. Great leaders clearly define and set expectations. And by constantly learning from success and setbacks, they effectively change people's limits and raise the bar.

#2: Vision

Vision is a clear and exciting picture of the future. Great leaders think big and challenge the norm. Always passionate, they have the courage to transform paradigms and policies to achieve desired results.

#3: Teamwork

Winning teamwork happens when a collaborative effort to achieve results exists. Great leaders create cultures of high trust and confidence. They create strong levels of commitment and accountability.

#4: Readiness

Readiness is the willingness to prepare and anticipate before acting. Great leaders ensure that the organization has the right people, the right processes, and the right tools in place to get results.

#5: Scorekeeping

Scorekeeping involves having a system for establishing and measuring progress. Great leaders keep score to win. They practice the 80/20 philosophy of focusing on the critical 20 percent of the measures that drive 80 percent of the success.

#6: Ownership
Ownership is the result of establishing authority, building commitment, and solidifying accountability. Great leaders execute projects with a sense of urgency. They also create a high-engagement culture in which everyone acts like an owner.

#7: Follow-Through
Follow-through is the discipline to finish tasks on schedule. Great leaders create a culture of reliability in which people can count on delivering high-quality results on time and on budget. They keep their eye on the ball.

#8: Focus
Focus is the ability to place relentless attention on top priorities. Great leaders focus on critical success factors, the vital few things that must go right to be successful. They empower teammates to operate in their "sweet spot" to perform at the highest level.

#9: Adaptability
Adaptability refers to flexibility and responsiveness to change. Great leaders understand that change is the only constant. As a result, they create a culture that supports taking calculated risks and is audible ready, capable of shifting the game plan at will as situations change.

#10: Communication
Communication is a skill that is developed through effective conversations. Realizing that effective communication is the number-one soft

skill to achieve excellence in execution, great leaders create cultures of integrity, encouraging open, candid discussion and debate.

Colin Powell said, "If you're going to achieve excellence in big things, you develop the habit in little matters." As we've analyzed our own journey and best practices across sports and business, we've distilled execution into ten actionable steps that can be integrated into your daily game plan.

With relentless focus, you can achieve excellence in execution, and we will show you how.

Execute to win!

René Vidal
Head Coach, McKendree
    University
rmvidal@mckendree.edu

Steve Finkelstein
Cofounder, Experience on Demand

steve@experience-on-demand.com

Execution Readiness Assessment

Top 10 Execution Skills	Major Issue 1	Issue 2	Good Shape 3	Excellent Shape 5
#1 – Leadership: We are achieving desired results. We set clear goals, expectations, and are fully engaged in the personal and professional development of our people. Our team members/employees are willing to be uncomfortable and have the courage to raise the performance bar.				
#2 – Vision: We have a clear and exciting picture of the future. We think big and challenge the norm. Each of our team members/employees has a personal vision and are committed and aligned to the team vision.				
#3 – Teamwork: We work collaboratively to achieve results. We have a culture of high trust, commitment, and accountability. We learn from both our successes and failures, constantly increasing our team's beliefs in the possibilities.				
#4 – Readiness: We prepare, plan, and anticipate before acting. Our team/organization has the right people, the right processes, and the right tools in place to get results. We have 90-day game plans to establish clarity of focus and inspire right action.				
#5 – Scorekeeping: We have a system for establishing expectations, measuring progress, and creating accountability. We proactively instill a winning mindset. We practice the 80/20 philosophy by focusing on the critical 20 percent of the measures that drive 80 percent of the success.				

#6 – Ownership: We empower people with the authority and responsibility to make decisions. We provide a sense of urgency in executing projects. We create a high-engagement culture in which everyone acts like an owner.				
#7 – Follow-Through: We have an execution discipline to finish tasks on schedule, on budget. Our word, actions, and winning habits are consistent, creating a culture of trust in meeting commitments.				
#8 – Focus: We place relentless attention on top priorities. We limit our priorities to the critical success factors – the vital few things that must go right. We practice mental discipline, eliminate distractions, and get into the "ZONE" to perform at the highest level.				
#9 – Adaptability: We are flexible and responsive to change. We understand that change is the only constant. We take calculated risks and are "audible-ready" to shift our game plan at will as situations change.				
#10 – Communication: We have effective, candid, and courageous conversations. We ask the right questions, listen, and collaborate to get to the best answers. We build ownership and commitment.				
Overall Execution Readiness				

CHAPTER 1

Leadership

The ability to get results

Challenge #1: Change People's Limits

> *The price of doing the same old thing is higher than the price of change.*
> —BILL CLINTON, FORTY-SECOND PRESIDENT OF THE UNITED STATES

Standards represent the level of excellence that you and your team consider the norm. As leader, you clearly establish what excellence looks like for your organization. Winning teams set clear expectations in tangible and intangible terms.

In fact, you likely began changing people's limits before you stepped into your leadership role. As a leader, this is who you are: *a perpetual change agent who constantly raises the bar on performance so that your team achieves excellence.*

Leaders never allow a "loss" to change the standard. When your standard is to be the best, you keep the bar set high. You guard against complacency and dips in intensity.

Also, you never allow a "win" to keep the standard. Maybe the bar was set too low. Standards are set to beat, not to meet.

In *The Winner Within*, legendary basketball coach Pat Riley writes, "Excellence is the gradual result of always striving to do better."

As a leader, what does personal excellence look like for you? How do you define excellence for your team or organization?

It's time to shatter all limitations for your organization and each member of your team.

Next Steps

☐ *Define your own success.*
☐ *Clarify success for your team or organization.*
☐ *Create a plan of attack.*

Challenge #2: Set Clear Goals

> *Working at the edge of what's challenging*
> *ensures we're always learning and growing.*
> —SUZANNE LANGLOIS, COFOUNDER,
> KALDIS COFFEE ROASTING COMPANY

Leaders focus on executing a few vital priorities well versus a lot of things just pretty good. To set worthy goals, use the Pareto principle: what are the 20 percent of the activities that make up 80 percent of the success?

In *Execution: The Discipline of Getting Things Done*, CEO Larry Bossidy says, "A leader who says 'I've got ten priorities' doesn't know what he's talking about."

Clear goals and prioritized lists have a huge influence on day-to-day execution. We've found that leaders who set too many objectives get lost in the fray, with great cost to productivity and results.

Specific goals have five key advantages:

1. Clarity—your team knows what to shoot for.
2. Focus—your team knows where to channel its energy.
3. Agility—your team learns how to navigate choppy waters.
4. Decisions—your team makes appropriate and informed trade-offs.
5. Productivity—your team excels with less effort and cost.

As a leader, what preconceived notions do you need to overcome? What are the exciting possibilities for your organization?

If you want to turn vision into reality, set clear, specific, time-keyed, and unified goals.

Next Steps

☐ *Project your team into the future.*
☐ *Create shared goals.*
☐ *Write down the benefits of achieving your goals.*
☐ *Review the consequences of noncompletion.*

Challenge #3: Engage Fully

> *Happy people give better performances.-*
> —TOMMY LASORDA, MANAGER, LOS ANGELES DODGERS

A leader who executes like a pro is vitally engaged in all aspects of "the program."

High-performance leadership occurs within the context of trusting relationships based on open communication, listening, understanding, caring, and respect.

Successful execution requires that leaders know their people and their business, including their strengths, weaknesses, passions, and dislikes.

Super Bowl champion Don Shula was known for being an "on the spot" leader. Shula prided himself on "never missing a play."

How about you? Are you in touch with the day-to-day realities of your craft? As a change maker, what's your level of personal engagement? Are your actions in alignment with your words?

Full engagement yields four core benefits:

1. Community—your team supports each other.
2. Ideation—your team produces fresh insights.
3. Momentum—your team takes relevant next steps.
4. Success—your team learns what it takes to pivot and excel.

The reality is that team members can feel and see your leadership presence.

Stoic philosopher Epictetus said, "The key is to keep company with people who uplift you, whose presence calls forth your best."

Winning leaders make sure their presence calls forth the very best from everyone, especially themselves.

Next Steps

☐ *Meet with the right people.*
☐ *Take time to listen.*
☐ *Create dialogue and connection through informality.*
☐ *Write personal notes, internally and externally.*

CHAPTER 2

Vision

A clear and exciting picture of the future

Challenge #4: Think Bigger

> *Employees need to connect what they
> do every day to a bigger purpose.*
> —LISA NICHOLS, CEO, TECHNOLOGY PARTNERS

L eaders create systems and procedures that are aligned with their vision of excellence.

Contrary to popular belief, champions rarely set out to break records. Rather, they view success as a by-product of hard work and smart thinking.

As a leader, everything you believe, say, and do is to prepare people to perform to the best of their ability. This begins by playing aggressively. Goethe said, "We will burn that bridge when we come to it."

Leaders talk and act in specific ways:

From Walt Disney: "If you can dream it, you can achieve it."
From President John F. Kennedy: "We choose to go to the moon this
decade."
From American leader Martin Luther King Jr.: "I have a dream."

In a homogenized world where mediocrity reigns, you can stand above it all by thinking big and having the courage of your convictions. Pretty good is never good enough.

What would you do if you had no limits? What would you do if you knew you wouldn't fail? Are you open to possibilities?

"I'll believe it when I see it" is really "I see it when I believe it." This is power of belief and thinking big.

Next Steps

☐ *Give yourself permission to dream.*
☐ *Identify and embrace fears, uncertainty, and discomfort.*
☐ *Commit to making your vision happen come hell or high water.*

Challenge #5: Create Your Personal Vision

My job is to prepare my players for life after softball.
—MIKE CANDREA, HEAD COACH, ARIZONA SOFTBALL
AND OLYMPIC GOLD MEDALIST

Vision is the change agent that shapes your personal growth, leadership influence, resilience, and organization for years to come.

The best visions are not only big and inspiring. They are personal. As we shared in *Play Smart to Win in Business*, "self-leadership precedes team leadership." Increase your own capacity to lead. Invest in yourself.

"The most powerful visions address and align your personal aspirations with your professional dreams," says Brian Moran, creator of *The 12 Week Year*.

A unique, personal, and compelling vision of the future

- creates movement and progress;
- drives emotional energy forward;
- helps push through discomfort; and
- enhances motivation and productivity.

What's your personal vision? What are you the most passionate about? What do you want to embody personally, spiritually, and emotionally? What kind of personal and professional relationships do you want to develop? What is a need in the marketplace that only you can fill?

The great Arthur Ashe said, "The doing is often more important than the outcome."

To move toward your vision, identify your next leadership action item.

Next Steps

- ☐ *Write down your short- and long-term aspirations.*
- ☐ *Define your three-year goals.*
- ☐ *Create your personal ninety-day strategic plan.*

Challenge #6: Chart the Team Vision

Teamwork is the essence of life.
—PAT RILEY, SEVEN-TIME NBA CHAMPION

Extraordinary leaders help their senior advisors, staff, players, and direct reports create a unified vision. What you want is a purpose-driven collective effort that executes for results.

As Steve Jobs said, "Great things in business are never done by one person. They're done by a team of people." Leaders who play to win get the right people on the bus in the right seats.

What do you want your team to look like? Have your team members shared their individual hopes for a better future? How will achieving your team vision change people's lives?

From our experience working with successful teams across sports and business, we've identified the following best practices:

- Winning teams are highly motivated.
- Winning teams know what achievement will enable.
- Winning teams commit to taking action.
- Winning teams create internal and external support systems.
- Winning teams own the results.
- Winning teams share lessons learned from success and failure.

Most importantly, a shared culture of team execution creates a "we're not afraid to lose" mind-set. You go after your goals with everything you've got. No excuses.

From Vince Lombardi: "Individual commitment to a group effort—that is what makes a team work, a company work, a society work, a civilization work."

Each team has to run its own race.

Is your team playing to win?

Next Steps

☐ Ask "Where do we want to go?"
☐ Draft a common team vision.
☐ Ask "What is our plan to get there?"
☐ Prioritize your team and individual goals.

CHAPTER 3

Teamwork

A collaborative effort to achieve results

Challenge #7: Develop Team Trust

> *Building strong, cohesive teams starts with trust.*
> —KELLY POLLOCK, EXECUTIVE DIRECTOR, COCA

E arvin Magic Johnson is a five-time NBA champion, a three-time NBA finals MVP, and a twelve-time NBA all-star. Magic believed that if he helped everyone around him get what they wanted out of the game of basketball, then winning would always follow.

Magic made all his teammates better.

What about you? How do you wake up the potential within your team? What are your beliefs around what makes a great team?

We've found that even the most talented teams can "hit the rim" when they get tripped up by the following issues:

- Constant infighting, turf wars, and rivalries
- Focus on individual versus team success

- Failure to acknowledge or understand potential threats
- Lack of trust
- Lack of accountability for results
- Lack of commitment to each other

Winning teamwork requires that everyone's efforts flow in a single direction. And this only happens in an environment of trust.

While people may be territorial animals, successful leaders create relational dynamics where team members harness their competitive leanings for the good of the team.

If it were easy to win a championship, everybody would be doing it. Yet as the great commander Hannibal said, "We will either find a way or make one."

With trust, you can effectively balance collaboration with a healthy competitive spirit.

How will you ensure that your team's efforts flow in the right direction?

Next Steps

☐ Complete the "Start, Stop, and Continue" exercise.
☐ Identify the strengths and limitations of your team members.
☐ Leverage strengths, and fortify weaknesses.

Challenge #8: Learn from Failure

Sometimes you win, sometimes you learn.
—JOHN MAXWELL, CEO, JOHN MAXWELL & CO.

In René's leadership conversation with culture-building expert Jon Gordon, Jon shared: "When driving change, make sure you honor your tradition, purpose, and culture. Generate power from your past to create your future."

On a global level, do you understand why teams fail to reach their potential? More specifically, what have you learned from the past, and how are you using that today to move your team, divisions, and company forward?

Winning leaders embody Michelangelo's famous saying *ancora imparo*, meaning "yet I am learning."

If you want to create a culture of execution, heed the following success distinctions, and tailor them to your leadership development program:

Losing Teams	Winning Teams
Do not keep score	Keep score
Do not prioritize culture	Make culture the number-one priority
Delegate culture building	Drive culture
Focus on outcomes and numbers	Focus on people and process
Feel no accountability for commitments	Assume accountability for results
Love to talk	Live the mission
Play it safe	Play to win
Create negaitivity	Generate positivity
Feel unprotected, vulnerable	Feel cared for, impenetrable

No one succeeds by doing the same thing over and over again and expecting a different result. You really can generate power from the past to create a better future.

Next Steps

☐ List one past "failure" experience.
☐ Complete the performance prompt "From this experience, we learned..."
☐ Ask as a team: "To improve our culture, what should be our next question?"

Challenge #9: Shape Your Team Beliefs

> *The moment you commit yourself,*
> *then Providence moves too.*
> —W. H. MURRAY, SCOTTISH MOUNTAIN CLIMBER

Beliefs drive action. The collective beliefs and habits of your team create results.

Is it time to change the attitude of your organization? If so, why is it imperative? Do you really want to create a culture of getting things done? What would be the benefits?

As a leader, your ability to inspire belief in your team members trumps all else. In fact, you can have the best talent, plans, strategy, and facilities and *still* come up short if you don't have belief.

Ultimately you want your team members to believe in themselves as much or more than you do.

Olympic champion Gail Devers said, "Keep your dreams alive. To achieve anything requires faith, belief in yourself, vision, hard work, determination, and dedication."

More than just a word or construct, belief is a mind-set.

Your number-one job as a leader is to inspire your team to believe. This includes motivation, but it doesn't end there. There is no finish line.

Leaders motivate, inspire, teach, and coach. You never stop raising the belief level of everyone around you. And you never stop sharing your belief with your team.

What beliefs do you most need now for the journey ahead? How can you share your beliefs in ways that stick?

Many leaders make the mistake of trying to change value systems. Core values are not the issue, nor are they in themselves a differentiator. Jack Welch said, "Integrity is just a ticket to the game."

Beliefs are the foundation of success. See and believe in the possibilities.

Change your team's beliefs to start executing like a pro team.

Next Steps

☐ *Express pride in your team.*
☐ *Praise and thank your team for who they are and what they do.*
☐ *Inspire your team with a compelling vision of the future.*

CHAPTER 4

Readiness

Prepare and anticipate before acting

Challenge #10: Get Ready to Play

> *Productivity is never an accident.*
> —PAUL J. MEYER, FOUNDER, SUCCESS
> MOTIVATION INSTITUTE

R eadiness is a state of total preparation. Winning leaders and organizations, like world-class athletes, move from the desire to win to *the will to prepare.*

It's the little things that make the big things happen.

For example, if you were to conduct a bag check of today's top tennis professionals, you'd find indispensable items such as

- extra racquets;
- extra clothing; and
- extra shoes, towels, water...

As a leader, what indispensable items do you have in your bag so that you can excel? Have you figured out the best approach to achieving your goals? Are you willing to do the work of preparation and take action?

"Most matches are won or lost well before you step on the court," writes professional women's tennis coach Nick Saviano in *Maximum Tennis*. The same principle applies to your life and work.

Leaders set the tone for the team by personal example and professional readiness.

When you work from a clear game plan, you will

- reduce mistakes;
- save time and resources;
- enhance focus; and
- win more than you lose.

Imagine executing a tennis strategy with the wrong equipment, while out of shape, or without the mind-set or belief that you can win.

Are you ready to play to win, or are you just practicing?

Next Steps

☐ *Schedule time to think about your goals.*
☐ *Map out the steps it will take to achieve your goals.*
☐ *Post your action items in your calendar.*

Challenge #11: Plan Twelve Weeks Out

I don't have a 3-5 year plan. My plan is day to day.
—DON SHULA, TWO-TIME SUPER BOWL CHAMPION

The legendary Don Shula recognized the difference between a vision and a plan. Shula's vision was one of perfection. He achieved the perfect season by leading his team to be great in the moment, one drill at a time, day by day.

In his *New York Times* best-selling book, *The 12 Week Year*, Brian Moran writes: "12 week planning is not quarterly planning, which is part of the outdated annualized thinking model. With 12 week planning, every 12 weeks stands alone; every 12 weeks is a new year and a chance to be great."

Planning twelve weeks out will help you and your team execute at the highest level. Results include the following:

- **Greater predictability.** It's easier to define the actions you need to execute in the next twelve weeks than it is over the next twelve months.
- **Greater focus.** It's easier to be great at the vital few than it is with the vicious many, to pursue the top one to three things that move your team forward.
- **Greater structure.** It's easier to game plan for short bursts than it is for long hauls.

We've found that failing to plan in "tighter compartments" is planning to fail, leading to "loose ends." Effective leaders commit to a positive sense of urgency.

Peter Drucker said, "Unless commitment is made, there are only promises and hopes, but no plans."

What major projects will you commit to for your next twelve weeks? Does your team have clarity on the projects that matter?

Next Steps

- ☐ *Establish your twelve-week goals.*
- ☐ *Identify your tactics.*
- ☐ *Prioritize 80/20 with relentless focus.*
- ☐ *Convey your expectations and build momentum.*

Challenge #12: Set Clear Expectations

People with clear, written goals achieve
far more in a shorter period of time.
—BRIAN TRACY, CEO, BRIAN TRACY INTERNATIONAL

If you don't know where you want your team to come out before you go in, you lose.

As a leader, what are the outputs that you're looking to create? What does your team physically have to produce to complete your project?

Be specific.

Our high-performance consulting and coaching work shows exactly why some leaders fall short on executing for results:

- They don't view planning time as productive time.
- They don't have clear weekly, daily, and hourly objectives.
- They don't bulletproof their team against distractions.

- They have too many objectives.
- They become frustrated, disillusioned, and less motivated.
- They have a numbers-based list without specific action items.

Actions tell the story. Outcomes win the Oscar.

Leaders understand that we have greater control over our actions than we do over our results. Focus on the steps and positive habits that lead to your desired outcome.

Are your tactics specific and actionable? Does your weekly plan include due dates and assigned responsibilities?

The marketplace rewards action and results, not intention or desire.

Henry Ford said, "You can't build a reputation on what you are going to do."

Next Steps

☐ *Determine your weekly outcomes.*
☐ *Delegate action items seven days in advance.*
☐ *Block your time strategically and relentlessly.*

CHAPTER 5

Scorekeeping

A system for establishing and measuring progress

Challenge #13: Instill a Winning Mind-Set

> *My dad encouraged us to fail.*
> —SARA BLAKELY, SPANX FOUNDER

I f you are not keeping score, you are only practicing.

The purpose of scorekeeping is to determine success and identify areas for improvement.

Moreover, scorekeeping is a mental game. Leaders understand the psychology of success and create cultures of mental toughness.

"Mind-set is everything," says X Prize chairman Peter Diamandis. "Mind-set influences the business and investment decisions you make, how you raise your children, and your overall well-being."

As a leader, how do you think about measurement? Are you keeping score or playing in the dark? How does your team know if they are winning or losing?

This chart identifies the mental blocks that can get in the way of executing to win:

Mental Blocks	Execute to Win
Fear measurement	Embrace realities
Focus solely on outcomes	Balance actions and results
"It's not my responsibility"	"I own this"
Cowardly and reactive	Courageous and proactive
Stop playing the game	Stay focused on task
Artificial motivation	Motivation based on progress

Leaders engage in scorekeeping in a way that positively impacts their team's productivity and results.

How are you framing the scorekeeping process for your team? Are you mentally preparing your team to win?

If you're not keeping score, you're not in the game.

Start keeping score to raise intensity, improve teamwork, and drive accountability throughout your organization. Focus on getting better and better each day, which can only happen through tracking.

This is your winning mind-set.

Next Steps

☐ Commit to keeping score.
☐ Establish both lead and lag indicators.
☐ Celebrate short-term wins.
☐ Focus on excellence, not perfection.

Challenge #14: Keep Score to Win

Learn the rules of the game, then
play better than anyone else.
—ALBERT EINSTEIN, THEORETICAL PHYSICIST

In professional tennis, players have visual access to three key metrics:

- Match score (e.g., two sets to one)
- Set score (e.g., five games to three)
- Game score (e.g., 40–love)

Also in view is content such as player names, home country, and serve mph—relevant data for the fans, not the players.

In our execution work, we've noted that CEOs and functional leaders often create scoreboards that "serve the leader, not the team." In actuality, you need both—a tracking system that positions both the leader and the team for success.

Unfortunately, problems occur under the following conditions:

- **The scorekeeping process is complicated.** People become overwhelmed.
- **The scoreboard overemphasizes lag indicators.** People don't know what they actually need to do to win.
- **The feedback isn't timely.** People aren't empowered to make game-time adjustments.

As a leader, you want to create excellence in execution. And an execution culture plays to win, not to lose.

Conventional Scoreboard Practice	Execute-to-Win Scoreboard Practice
Presents complex, rich data	Presents simple, relevant data
Is nonexistent or hidden	Is visible
Not valued as important	Drives accountability
Offers insufficient measures	Offers lead and lag metrics
Results in delay, confusion	Ensures timely feedback, clarity
Engenders apathy, indifference	Inspires full engagement

What are the behaviors of a fully engaged team? Are the team's metrics easily identifiable and measureable?

Venus Williams, who wisely leveraged her tennis ability into entre-preneurial success, said, "I don't focus on what I'm up against. I focus on my goals and ignore the rest."

What does it take for your team to win?

Next Steps

☐ Track lead and lag indicators.
☐ Position your scoreboard where everyone can see and understand it.
☐ Provide real-time feedback.

Challenge #15: Take Small Steps Daily

Words are cheap. Actions matter.
—CHARLES CHAPUT, AMERICAN
PRELATE, CATHOLIC CHURCH

Your team embraces execution. You understand and are committed to the metrics that drive results. You are now measuring execution on a daily basis, which begs further inquiry:

Are you doing what you said is important to achieve your goals?
Are you executing with excellence on your top goals?
Are you effective or not? Are you efficient or not?
Is your team winning or losing?

The surest route to mediocrity is inconsistency. What you want as an exceptional leader is to execute your fundamentals on a daily basis. Winning teams take the right steps each day until they become automatic.

Ironically, in sports, business, and life, the less thinking you have to do under pressure, the better you will perform. When your day-to-day activities are aligned with your vision, you will love your results.

Winning teams and companies are action oriented. "Focus on what it takes to be successful," says renowned coach Nick Saban. "Your culture is an accumulation of your thoughts, habits, and priorities on a day-to-day basis."

As a leader, you know you're achieving excellence in execution when you see

- informed decision-making;
- higher team confidence and collaboration;

- better systematic projections of next steps;
- improved productivity and performance;
- greater focus and resiliency;
- performers scoring themselves; and
- ownership around outcomes and adaptability.

Excellence is a gradual result of always striving to get better. It's a hallmark of every business leader, best-selling author, and Olympic champion that we interviewed on execution for results.

What steps can you take today toward excellence?

Next Steps

- ☐ *Score your execution.*
- ☐ *Confront any lack of execution.*
- ☐ *Raise your level of execution each day.*
- ☐ *Build confidence through success and trust through failure.*

CHAPTER 6

Ownership

Establishing authority, building commitment and accountability

Challenge #16: Create a Burning Platform

> *People in this organization will be known*
> *for meeting commitments. Period.*
> —LARRY BOSSIDY, CEO, ALLIEDSIGNAL

What would be different and better for your team if everyone operated with a positive sense of urgency? What are the barriers to achieving a sense of urgency?

Imagine a culture where you have a fast flow of useful information to streamline processes, raise necessity, and improve execution.

The Twenty-Five-Second Rule

In professional tennis, you have twenty-five seconds, not twenty-five years, to compete and win. Players literally have twenty-five seconds between points to process what just happened and plan for what happens next.

Choice, consequence, and time limits always prevail in the lives of top performers.

As a leader, are you creating a burning platform? Is your team playing with a sense of healthy desperation?

"No leader has five years in business," says Alan Weiss, best-selling author of *Million-Dollar Consulting*. "In five years you fall behind. You have to begin right now, this minute."

Here are three quick steps you can take to create a burning platform and ignite team ownership:

1. Describe how the platform is burning.
2. Define why your team should "take the flames seriously."
3. Communicate next steps for change and future possibilities.

Tolstoy said, "The two most powerful warriors are patience and time." Or, as we advise our clients, "Have quick feet and slow hands."

Next Steps

☐ *Set tight deadlines.*
☐ *Don't procrastinate.*
☐ *Describe potential negative consequences.*
☐ *Provide freedom to thrive.*

Challenge #17: Build Collective Pride

*Do common things in an uncommon ways and
you will command the world's attention.*
—George Washington Carver,
American botanist and inventor

Imagine if everyone came to work engaged. What if everyone acted like an owner?

How would your culture improve if every member of your team did everything to the best of their ability? Not because they had to, but because they wanted to?

Leaders don't hire disengaged employees. Disconnect happens when pride isn't consistently built and reinforced throughout the culture.

It becomes the leader's team rather than a collective mission.

Team members genuinely want to put their personal signatures on everything they do. Thus, winning leaders build collective pride.

Pride is doing something to the best of your ability because it's a reflection of you. Pride is self-respect. It's about who you are as a leader—on the court or in the corner office.

Pride is also the feeling of gratification your team gets by being part of something bigger than themselves. It's team dignity.

John Steinbeck wrote, "I am impelled, not to squeak like a grateful and apologetic mouse, but to roar like a lion out of pride in my profession."

Take a moment to think about your most memorable leadership moments.

Likely your greatest memories revolve around team success, family experiences, and community impact. Pride in team matters.

In what ways does your team uphold group standards? Does the team belong to just one person, a clique, or everyone?

How can you build collective pride?

<u>**Next Steps**</u>

☐ *Make a personal commitment: "I will do my best."*
☐ *Make a team commitment: "The team belongs to all of us."*
☐ *Go all in as a team: "We win and we lose together."*

Challenge #18: Coach to Win

> *Your title makes you a manager. Your*
> *people decide if you're a leader.*
> —BILL CAMPBELL, LEGENDARY SILICON VALLEY ADVISOR

It's no secret that society's highest achievers have coaches. The right coaching can build extraordinary confidence, double productivity, and dramatically improve execution.

Without great coaching, companies and teams limit the results they produce.

What would've happened to Apple if they hadn't brought back Steve Jobs?

Roger Federer, regarded by many fans, peers, and analysts as the greatest tennis player of all time, has sought advice from a variety of coaches and mentors.

How far will your team get without a great coach? And how far can you go with a great one?

"The best coaches have experience, can manage the team, and serve as visionaries," says Andy Andrews, author of *The Traveler's Gift* and consultant to several BCS national football champions.

Five Secrets of High-Performance Coaching

1. **Keep winning and losing in perspective.** Make good events better. Transform bad events into opportunities to learn.
2. **Lead by example.** Your own preparation and conduct must be exemplary.
3. **Go for respect over popularity.** Focus on courage and getting things done.
4. **Value character as well as ability.** Find out what makes your players tick.
5. **Work hard, and enjoy what you do.** Create an environment where people can do the best work of their lives.

Sometimes people need just a little bit of coaching for great things to happen.

Next Steps

☐ _Create a high-performance coaching culture._
☐ _Increase your team's awareness by identifying its strengths and weaknesses._
☐ _Position your players to win by playing to their strengths._

CHAPTER 7

Follow-Through

The discipline to finish tasks on schedule

Challenge #19: Be Consistent

> *Exceptional leaders build trust with people*
> —HELEN JARDINE, CHIEF DEVELOPMENT OFFICER,
> NORTHWESTERN MUTUAL

Tough-love coaching: your people don't follow through because you don't follow through. You chose talent over character, expediency over effectiveness, and popularity over respect.

The good news is that reliability not only can be restored, it will become stronger than ever if you commit 100 percent to becoming more consistent.

Relationships are built on trust and respect. And few relationships are as important as the ones among members of your team.

Leaders build great relationships by forming and honoring agreements. Agreements come in all shapes and sizes, but the most important agreements are the ones you make with yourself.

This is key to creating a culture of follow-through and execution.

Inconsistent leaders

- *don't delegate; they're always "in the weeds";*
- *don't keep agreements;*
- *don't embrace confrontation;*
- *lose trust;*
- *lose authority;*
- *cost the organization time, focus, and money;*
- *distrust themselves; and*
- *disrespect the team!*

EXECUTION LEADERS, *on the other hand,*

- *delegate like pros;*
- *honor agreements; they do what they say;*
- *face the brutal facts;*
- *earn trust daily;*
- *gain and maintain respect;*
- *steward resources wisely;*
- *lead with personal power; and*
- *respect everyone's time.*

As a leader, how many agreements have you recently broken to yourself or to others? Einstein said, "Whoever is careless with the truth in small matters cannot be trusted with important matters."

One of the leadership lessons René learned while coaching at the College of William & Mary was that "your team is always watching you."

What kind of example are you setting? Are you building dependability through consistency?

Next Steps

- ☐ *Make fewer agreements.*
- ☐ *Learn how to say no, and say no more often.*
- ☐ *Renegotiate commitments you can't keep.*
- ☐ *Get your team's agreement on follow-through ground rules.*

Challenge #20: Create Follow-Through Mechanisms

Follow-through is the cornerstone of execution.
—RAM CHARAN, GLOBAL BUSINESS ADVISOR

In sports, the perfect follow-through is the result of all the proper mechanics that occurred before the finish. In basketball, perhaps it's getting your feet set. In volleyball, maybe it's your serve toss.

In business, winning leaders execute follow-through with excellence. In fact, they are "follow-through fanatics." Leaders who achieve excellence in execution don't only set directives—they stick around to realize them.

"Many people don't focus enough on execution. If you make a commitment to get something done, you need to follow through on that commitment," says Ken Chenault, former CEO and chairman at American Express.

Once leaders embrace an initiative, they make sure it's put into effect. It's not an experiment.

Consistent, reliable follow-through

1. ensures people are doing the things they committed to do;
2. ensures people are assigned in a manner aligned with their strengths;
3. makes certain people are on timetable and monitored frequently;
4. exposes lack of discipline; and
5. increases specificity and unlocks agility.

As a leader, do you have clear conclusions about who does what and when? Have you put names to those who are accountable for results? Is everybody carrying away the right information and taken ownership for what he or she has agreed to do?

To achieve excellence in execution, create simple follow-through mechanisms:

- One-on-one conversations
- Group settings
- Written letters confirming agreements made

Clear, continuous, and relevant dialogue calibrates people's expectations, aligns the team, and fosters leadership development.

Remember, It's not where you start. It's how you finish that matters most.

Next Steps

☐ *Surface any conflicts standing in the way of results.*
☐ *Clarify who does what and when.*
☐ *Name those accountable for results.*
☐ *Track and report progress and outcomes.*
☐ *Glean lessons learned via "nameless, shameless debriefs."*

Challenge #21: Finish the Match

You can't run out the clock. You must finish.
—ANDRE AGASSI, EIGHT-TIME GRAND
SLAM TENNIS CHAMPION

Ivan Lendl, known as "the Tennis Terminator," understood how to quickly bring competition to a close. You never wanted to fall behind Lendl, because he knew how to build on a lead and finish you off.

Ultimately, success is getting the job done—*finishing the match.*

How good is your team at finishing? Are you trying to play catch-up, or are you ahead of the game? What kind of unfinished business is lurking in the shadows?

How to Finish Like a Champion

1. Continue to achieve your short-term milestones.
2. Focus on the process, not the score.
3. Brainwash yourself into believing the game is about effort, not the end result.
4. Have the "ball on your racquet"—control your own destiny.
5. Keep earning. "Every point is like money in the bank. Great closers play the way they've played throughout the match," says Fed Cup coach Lynne Rolley.
6. Stay tactically focused in the present.

Nothing builds confidence like a successful finish.

Louis Zamperini, one of America's greatest heroes and Olympians, said, "That's one thing you learn in sports. You don't give up; you fight to the finish."

How does the principle of finishing apply to your organization?

Next Steps

- ☐ Identify the cost of complacency.
- ☐ Review the benefits of executing on plan.
- ☐ Focus on the process, not the score.

CHAPTER 8

Focus

Relentless attention on top priorities

Challenge #22: Limit Your Priorities

> *The skill of prioritizing is one of the most underrated*
> *skills of the world's most highly successful people.*
> —DR. JASON SELK, AUTHOR,
> *ORGANIZE TOMORROW TODAY*

Most teams overemphasize the goal-setting process and don't focus on what needs to be done to accomplish goals.

In sports, every organization has the same goal: win the Super Bowl, get the ring, skate to the Stanley Cup. But it's focus—the day-to-day observation, monitoring, and follow-up—that makes it happen.

Unfortunately, too many companies get overwhelmed by scattering their focus.

As a leader, do you have too many balls in the air? What's your most important project? Out of the myriad choices under consideration, what has the highest probability of success?

Winning teams add and subtract from the plan until they have their "short list." They eliminate wasteful activity and focus on the vital few.

Five Tips for World-Class Prioritization

1. Clarify your most valuable priorities (MVPs).
2. Make sure your MVPs are your own, not someone else's.
3. Begin each day with a game plan.
4. Align your commitments (yeses) to your MVPs.
5. Say no to easier projects that don't move the needle forward.

Inventor Alexander Graham Bell said, "Concentrate all your thoughts upon the work at hand. The sun's rays do not burn until brought to a focus."

By channeling your focus and energy, you will execute like a pro on your top priorities and raise performance to the highest level.

Next Steps

☐ *Play to your strengths.*
☐ *Commit to a stop-doing list.*
☐ *Take time to unplug.*

Challenge #23: Get into the Flow

Competition is an easy way to get into flow.
—MIHALY CSIKSZENTMIHALYI, HUNGARIAN-
AMERICAN PSYCHOLOGIST

You want your team's energy going toward playing their best. As a winning leader, you're in the business of eliminating interferences so that your players can get into the zone.

This is where high performance is possible. Competing on autopilot allows you to achieve excellence in execution.

Leaders don't want

- players worried about their assignments;
- tentative decision-making, play, and social interaction; or
- distracting mechanical trifles.

"The goal of the autopilot concept in business is to free people up to do on their own what they've learned reflects the values, goals, and standards of the company," says management consultant Ken Blanchard.

Does your team know its patterns forward and backward? As a leader, are you able to improvise and be creative in ways that enhance your performance? Do your players have the ability to coach themselves?

Great things happen when your team knows the playbook inside and out. Thinking about mechanics and worrying about the future undermines performance.

Our leadership research and execution work further proves that productivity skyrockets when leaders are in the flow.

What can you do to get in the zone?

Next Steps

☐ *Give your team "the playbook."*
☐ *Help your team master its assignments.*
☐ *Foster your team's ability to coach itself.*

Challenge #24: Practice Mental Discipline

Elite athletes don't leave any stone unturned.
—DR. JIM AFREMOW, AUTHOR, *THE CHAMPION'S MIND*

Whereas mental toughness is about resilience and bouncing back from adversity, *mental discipline* is about proactivity and extreme focus.

The unnoticed error will bury you. As a leader, if you let errors go unheeded, you'll ensure that more of them occur.

Winning leaders execute for results by building teams that

- make few errors; and
- learn from those errors.

Every mistake is an opportunity to learn something you don't want to repeat.

When teams lose focus and mental discipline, they run into problems:

- Crisis—moving from one event to another without reflection
- Denial—looking away from errors rather than toward them
- Fear—fearing what an error may say about character or competence

You want to develop a reputation for consistency in execution. When René asked cancer survivor Jerry Kill what made Tom Brady great, the championship football coach replied, "Brady doesn't make mistakes."

Three Keys to Mental Discipline

1. Analyze every play, and learn everything you can from it.
2. Notice and correct every mistake on the spot.
3. Emphasize execution and progress.

In sports, a *crisp* practice usually leads to excellence in execution. In business, there is no practice.

In what ways can you apply the principle of focus to accomplishing your goals?

Next Steps

☐ *Observe performance daily.*
☐ *Affirm positive performance.*
☐ *Don't settle for subpar performance.*

CHAPTER 9

Adaptability

Flexibility and responsiveness to change

Challenge #25: Lead, Don't Follow

> *You can't build an adaptable organization*
> *without adaptable people.*
> —GARY HAMEL, FOUNDER, STRATEGOS

J ust as tennis players move forward, backward, and laterally to win matches, business leaders must be agile enough to succeed in the marketplace.

Brad Gilbert, former top-five tennis-touring professional and coach to Andre Agassi, kept a diary on the habits and tendencies of every ranked competitor. As a result, Gilbert facilitated his ability to mentally and physically adapt *before* the match begun.

To improve his own execution, Gilbert understood that "one cannot manage change; one can only be ahead of it."

"Execution-oriented companies change faster than others because they are closer to the situation," says business author Ram Charan.

As a leader, what are you doing to stay ahead of change?

Three Tips for Leading Change

1. Pay attention to detail. Little things make big things happen.
2. Deal with negatives early. Little things can quickly become big things.
3. Focus on people details. Adaptable people drive agile cultures.

By staying close to the action, you will

- gain the competitive edge;
- thrive in difficult times; and
- generate better results.

USC professor Leo Buscaglia said, "Change is the end result of all true learning."

It's not enough to be a student of success. You must create a culture of "practitioners."

What's the level of collective awareness within your organization? As a top performer, what must you study, learn, and integrate to lead change?

It's what leaders learn after they know it all that counts.

Next Steps

☐ *Identify and root out negativity.*
☐ *Brainstorm the possibilities.*
☐ *Adapt what you do to who you are and where you want to go.*

Challenge #26: Take Prudent Risks

Risk comes from not knowing what one is doing.
—WARREN BUFFET, CEO, BERKSHIRE HATHAWAY

Winning leaders are not afraid of losing or trying new things.

Everybody talks about change, but few leaders actually take prudent risks and *change* what they do.

Because old habits can be stronger than the desire to change, many leaders are prone to

- miss opportunities;
- slow decision-making cycles; and
- act as if nothing is happening.

As a leader, are you willing to develop new skills and capacities? Have you observed what the "new players" are doing in similar industries? How can you turn a negative into a positive initiative for change?

How to Experiment Like a Pro
We've found that winning teams thrive when they

1. quickly read and act on marketplace signals;
2. experiment rapidly;
3. learn from experience;
4. iterate in real time; and
5. engage in continual skill and leadership development.

Truly adaptable teams also experiment at a faster pace than others, at a lower cost, and with broader scope. They are also tolerant of inherent failure. In fact, failure is celebrated.

"It is only a failure if we fail to get the learning," says Scott Cook, cofounder of Intuit.

If you're not failing, you're not trying.

What new tactics can you employ for success? How is the changing marketplace influencing your decision-making? Are you prepared to adjust in real time?

Next Steps

☐ *Develop new skills.*
☐ *Experiment rapidly.*
☐ *Learn from failure.*

Challenge #27: Be Audible Ready

> *The secret to success is to be ready*
> *when your opportunity comes.*
> —BENJAMIN DISRAELI, TWO-TIME
> BRITISH PRIME MINISTER

Rigid game plans are deadly. Nothing stays the same.

Too often a leader will hold on to a game plan that no longer works. As a result, they get caught flat footed, consumed by circumstances, and begin to second-guess themselves.

According to Cambridge physicist Stephen Hawking, "intelligence is the ability to adapt to change."

As a leader, you want to be able to shift your game plan at will. Why? Because the teams that constantly adapt are the teams that win.

It's vital that you expect the unexpected and reserve your right to change as new events emerge. Whether it's a tweak or a total overhaul, you must be prepared to call audibles.

Audibles are well-thought-out and choreographed plays ahead of time. It's the ability to substitute new assignments and tactics for the ones you prepared to perform.

How to Be Audible Ready

1. Continually scan for new data.
2. Become a "what if" person.
3. Identify and anticipate obstacles.
4. Have the necessary resources on hand.
5. Be open to changing as necessary to get the job done.
6. Implement without looking back.
7. Focus on what happens next.

Do you have the ability to adjust to the times? Are you open to change? How do you develop top performers to navigate through seas of change?

Winning leaders can substitute plays at will in order to get the job done.

Next Steps

☐ Anticipate obstacles.
☐ Secure resources.
☐ Implement decisively.

CHAPTER 10

Communication

The ability to have effective conversations

Challenge #28: Become a Master Communicator

> *The single biggest problem in communication*
> *is the illusion it has taken place.*
> —BERNARD SHAW, IRISH PLAYWRIGHT

American investor Warren Buffet is famous for his prudent investment analysis. In fact, Buffet's intensive preparation also encompasses spending considerable time with key people in an organization.

Buffet asks himself three questions regarding core leaders:

1. Do I like them?
2. Do I trust them?
3. Do I respect them?

If the answer to any one of these questions is no, the deal is off.

In René's research on the success of Notre Dame basketball, the data pointed to head men's coach Mike Brey's talent as a *master communicator.* To execute like a pro, apply the following best practices to your most important projects.

Elements of Master Communication

- You understand your audience.
- You show respect by listening.
- You have a communication strategy and plan.
- You are open and honest.
- You are proactive, not reactive.
- You are clear and concise, and you communicate often.
- You simplify the content—"less is more."
- You choose the right medium.

"The first rule of business is not to lose. The second rule is not to forget the first rule," says Buffet.

By investing the time to listen to others, to understand and meet needs, you set the stage for productive conversations that lead to results.

Leaders who play to win master the art of communication.

Next Steps

- ☐ *Prepare for your audience.*
- ☐ *Be clear and concise.*
- ☐ *Become a great listener.*
- ☐ *Be proactive, not reactive.*

Challenge #29: Don't Play Games

Be candid with everyone.
—JACK WELCH, CEO, GENERAL ELECTRIC

Integrity means being honest with yourself and others.

Winning Leaders speak and live the truth. The research is clear: *people need and want honesty in a leader.* Employees want to be told the truth. They don't appreciate or respect leaders who "go around corners."

In fact, the number-one characteristic people are looking for in a leader is integrity.

Effective leaders are clear and straightforward. As a result of this approach

- they develop and maintain good relationships;
- their players expect candor from them; and
- they achieve congruence between shared values and organizational behavior.

As a leader, are you straight with your people? Can your team expect direct, just, and candid communication?

Leaders don't play games. Their own high self-concept won't allow for anything less.

The great John Wooden said, "There is no pillow as soft as a clear conscience."

We continually find that what an effective leader says and does is the same. Integrity and peace of mind are intangibles that cannot be measured by a win-loss record or the latest sales report.

Three Quick Communication Tips

1. Confront your people.
2. Praise people sincerely.
3. Provide constructive feedback.

Being straightforward is the fast track to communicating effectively, building trust, and executing like a pro.

Next Steps

☐ *Approach things in a straightforward way.*
☐ *Value and respect honesty in others.*
☐ *Solve problems quickly. Don't let problems fester.*

Challenge #30: Have Conversations

> *A long walk and a calm conversation are an incredible combination if you want to build a bridge.*
> —SETH GODIN, AUTHOR, *LINCHPIN*

Communication is just as important, if not more so, than technical ability.

By modeling true dialogue and collaboration, winning leaders create positive learning environments that execute for results.

- The team communicates well under pressure.
- Corrections are made immediately.
- Top performers share secrets of success.
- Different viewpoints are sought and valued.
- Individual credibility makes the team stronger.

Leaders get into trouble when they assume communication is taking place.

Amateur communicators...	*Execution leaders...*
Don't ask questions	*Ask great questions*
Have no system in place	*Have good systems*
Take talking for granted	*Create dialogue*
Act as introverts under pressure	*Get issues on the table*
Have too many meetings	*Communicate instantly*
Stop and overanalyze	*Decide and start*
Hire technical skills only	*Hire great communicators*

Leaders always search for the communicators on the team. By word and example, they also remind people to talk, use repetition to reinforce, and ensure that only the truth is spoken.

Where are the communicators on your team? In what ways are you teaching your team to engage in real collaboration? Are you gaining valuable input on successes, weaknesses, opportunities, and potential threats?

Elon Musk said, "It's very important to have a feedback loop, where you're constantly thinking about what you've done and how you could be doing it better."

What's *your* feedback loop telling you? Are you teaching your team how to talk?

<u>Next Steps</u>

☐ *Ask your "players" for ongoing feedback.*
☐ *Create a communication system and rhythm.*
☐ *Create a culture where people want to talk to each other.*

CONCLUSION

We have done our best in these pages to make this book rich in application. As a result, what is a slender volume is still packed with strategies, tactics, and practical checklists. Yet, the basic message is simple: *Winning leaders articulate a vision and make it real. This is the essence of execution.*

A Template for Execution

1. Great leaders achieve excellence in execution.
2. Great leaders turn dreams into reality.
3. Great leaders leverage the power of teams.
4. Great leaders create luck through preparation.
5. Great leaders keep score to win.
6. Great leaders create a culture of ownership and accountability.
7. Great leaders finish what they start.
8. Great leaders are relentlessly focused on core objectives.
9. Great leaders are role models for adaptability.
10. Great leaders empower others through effective communication.

The world's wisdom traditions teach that implementation is the key to building successful lives and businesses. Hillel the Elder said, "Who does not grow, declines," then asked, "If I am not for others, what am I? If not now, when?" By rising to the challenges we have presented in this book, we are confident that you will empower others as you empower yourself, unlocking the potential of greatness that resides in us all.

Only through action can you bring a vision to life.

LEADERSHIP CONVERSATION WITH MIKE CANDREA

USA SOFTBALL OLYMPIC GOLD & SILVER MEDALIST

Provided by CoachVidal.com

Mike Candrea is the head softball coach at the University of Arizona in Tucson, Arizona. He was the head coach of the United States women's national softball team in 2004, when Team USA won a gold medal, and in 2008, bringing home silver. Under Candrea, the Arizona softball team has won eight NCAA Women's College World Series titles. (The following content represents Coach Mike Candrea's own words.)

Mental Toughness is Power

My dad was a jazz musician. We gravitated from White Plains, New York to New Orleans, Louisiana. That was because of my dad's music – he played in some big bands, and when he was in the service, he was in charge of the USO shows. On a trip to New Orleans to perform, he met my mom.

My dad was a full-blooded Italian and my mom's French, which makes for a great combination...terrific food growing up! However, the reality is that my dad lived a different life, and although he taught me a lot of valuable lessons, I knew I didn't want his lifestyle.

> *My dad taught me about hard love. When I went off to college, he handed me twenty bucks and said, "Good luck." The lesson was, "Mike, if you're going to make it in life, you're going to have to make it on your own." You can't count on anyone else. My dad gave me mental toughness.*

My mom was the key influencer in my faith. A very strong woman, my mom took me to Catechism class every Sunday. When I raised my kids, I gave them an option, which I wish I'd never done. Now however, they understand how important it is to have spiritual consistency in your life.

Each of my parents had a huge influence on me, yet not as much as you might think regarding the world of sports. Though I watched my dad play softball as a kid, I never thought that I'd be coaching fast pitch softball someday. All I remember was fighting mosquitos off every night (in Louisiana) watching him play.

Additional lessons I learned from my parents:

- **The Power of Humility.** I grew up a very humble young man.
- **The Power of Self-Discipline.** My dad believed, *"Nothing good ever happens after midnight."* Eleven p.m. was my curfew. My dad was unique because he would set the alarm for eleven p.m. in his bedroom, and I had to be in on time to turn that thing off or I'd be in deep trouble!
- **The Power of Self-Maturity.** When I was a little kid, I'd follow my dad around as he was mowing the lawn. As a teenager, I thought he was dumbest S.O.B in the world. Then, as I got older, I followed my parents' model of creating a loving family.
- **The Power of Family.** Every holiday, we celebrate as a family together. When my dad retired, and my mom and dad went back to New Orleans to take care of my grandmother, my mom took care of her mom every day for thirteen years. That just doesn't happen today. I told them that one day, *"When grandma passes away, I'm going to build a house for you on my (Arizona) property so we can have coffee every day."* They lived with me for many years before my dad passed away.

Success is a Process

I was a junior college baseball player. After I hurt my elbow, I was asked to help coach. I was blessed to be amongst some very good coaches through the baseball coaching association. I was able to listen to some really quality people and pull wisdom nuggets from everyone.

Later on in my career, my biggest influence was George Young. George was the athletic director (and coach of seven different sports) at Central Arizona College and a four-time Olympian. I had a chance to work for George and to also watch him train—seeing George break the four-minute mile in his thirties. He was a remarkable athlete that got up every morning, ran his 6-7 miles out in the desert. There was no one around or watching. Then, George would do the same thing in the evenings. I really learned what competition was all about.

> *"Every time the alarm rings, I think about the Russians getting up and doing their workout. That's what keeps me going."*
> —GEORGE YOUNG, FOUR-TIME OLYMPIAN

George was a driven individual who not only taught me how to compete but not to worry about the things you don't have. Do the best with what you have. We can always sit around and complain about what we'll never have. It's not about how much money you have, your budget, or the school you're at, but taking the people you have and making them the best they can be. That philosophy really had an impact on me.

He was also one of those guys who would take a kid off of the reservation – a distance runner for example – and through hard work each morning, that kid would become a very good runner. So George was one of the first leaders who really made me think about the process. If there is anything that's a process, it's distance running. You're doing it every day under different conditions every time you're out there. The big thing is that nobody is out there to watch you. You can cut corners, do whatever you want, and not have the discipline you need but ultimately it will come out in a loss.

George also gave me an idea of what the Olympics is all about. I never dreamed I'd be in the Olympics. In the 1980s and 1990s, softball wasn't even in the Olympics.

> *With the Olympics, I realized that you're practicing*
> *for four years for one moment in time. You have*
> *one opportunity to put it all together.*

Therefore, the process becomes very important in that situation. These experiences made me a very process-oriented person, not worrying about the end result. The daily question I ask of myself and our team is: *"What do we need to do today in our plan to get better?"*

Coach Candrea's Five Coaching Pillars

As a coach in today's world I've recently done something that I've never done before. I gave every kid a blank uniform. The culture has changed so much that I felt when we put on the "A" (for Arizona), we really didn't know what it represents. During the last few years, we've been battling a lack of leadership. As a result, we decided that the players need to earn the "A."

Our 5 pillars for success are:

1. **Character.** If I can make the student-athletes better people, then they'll become better players.
2. **Attitude.** You have control of your attitude every day. Are you going to be a great teammate?

3. **Discipline.** To be successful at anything in life, you have to have discipline. Discipline in your preparation. Discipline in your personal readiness to play the game. Discipline in your skill development.
4. **Performance.** To be able to perform, you have to be consistent in every aspect of the game.
5. **Teamwork.** Communication skills are a lot different today. We invest a significant amount of discussing what it takes to be a great teammate and how to elevate others. How can you be a consistently good teammate on a day-to-day basis?

Leadership is a Skill

In the early 1990s, when we were on a constant roll, we had student-athletes who grew up a little bit differently. They didn't have all the choices in life that we have today. Nor did they have the distractions.

Social media has changed the world of sports.

Back in the day, we always had kids that would rise to the occasion, step up, and be accountable. I feel that, in the last three years, the people who I thought would be good leaders have turned out not to be very good leaders. As a result, our current focus is on developing better leaders.

In the very first meeting of the year, I had the kids rank each other from one through nineteen on who they thought were the top leaders on the team. Then, I took the top 10 and we brought them to a leadership conference to give them some ideas and skills of what a leader really is. We think this will be very helpful for us. We're also blessed at Arizona to have several performance, leadership, and coaching experts on staff to assist in the leadership development of our players.

The players on this year's team have responded positively to some of our adjustments. Ultimately, every player goes through the leadership training. I also have conversations with each player, particularly those individuals who were ranked at the bottom of the leadership scale. I say:

"This is what your peers think. The goal is for you to climb this ladder because many of you have leadership skills but you're not using them. What's keeping you from using your leadership skills?"

I've never had Captains on my team. Our approach has been that everyone should be able to lead in her own way. As a leader, you can't sit back and think that everybody is going to rise to the top.

An important distinction I've learned from coaching females athletes for thirty-plus years is this:

Men have to play good to feel good. Women have to feel good to play good.

Therefore, the emotional piece is a huge part for the female athlete. The objective is to get the players to separate the emotions from the real topic.

Adaptability is Key

One of the first lessons I learned coaching internationally was to always expect the unexpected. No matter where we went. I could have the perfect practice plan. Yet the unexpected would occur. For example, on a trip to the Dominican Republic for the Pan Am Games, I prepared a practice plan and walked in thinking they're going to have a facility like we have at Arizona. Well, I stumble upon this pasture, with very little dirt and a couple of donkeys tied up in left field!

*We learned quickly that we would have to
adapt to what the situation warrants.*

As Americans, we run our lives by the clock. In Beijing, it was quite different. We'd be urgently travelling to a game and get stuck behind someone driving five miles per hour, trying to play mind games with us. Little incidents such as these helped us become much more adaptable to change and conflict.

Thus, we began creating highly pressurized practice scenarios. For example, our staff asked the bus driver to fake as if the bus wouldn't start. We arrived to the game late and had to compete without the benefit of warming up.

Handling distractions was a huge challenge at the Olympics. Usually the distractions came from parents and family members. It's probably the reason we have the Olympic Village, so the parents can stay somewhere else.

As a coach, what I learned is that most of the time when a performance goes bad at the Olympics, it's because people change. They think they have to do something different. Of course, pressure gets to everyone a little bit differently.

*One of the things I tried to do as an Olympic coach
was to make sure every game looked the same.*

Top Performers Embrace Challenge

When dealing with athletes, if you have low skill athletes in a high skill challenge, they get frustrated. By the same token, if you high skill athletes in a low skill challenge, they get bored. So with the Olympics gold-medal team, I really had to challenge them every day in practice. When we did that, the players loved it.

I used to sit and pause for a moment to ask, *"What makes these gold-medal kids so different?"* Here are the answers I came up with:

- **Emotional Stability.** They never got too high or too low.
- **Consistency.** They looked the same at practice as they did in the Olympic arena.
- **World-Class Practice Habits.** They trained at a very high level.
- **Mental and Physical Skills.** It was the first time I was able to watch kids in the sport play at their peak—at twenty-seven or twenty-eight years old. It was phenomenal to watch.

In the first meeting with our 2004 team, I said, *"I didn't want to just win a gold medal. I wanted to dominate the world."* They all kind of looked at me like, *"Who the hell are you?"* But I felt that if we had a good training process, that this team could play the very best softball you'd have ever seen, and they did.

In 2008 (when we earned the silver medal), I thought our process was very good. It really was not much different than our gold medal 2004 team process. We had a few more distractions in 2008. The almighty dollar got in the way of some decisions we had to make; trying to pay our athletes as much as we could to keep them happy for example. Truthfully, the only thing I can say that was different is that we ran into a very hot pitcher from Japan. There's nothing I look back on and regret or would have done differently.

> *On any given day, you can be beat. It's part of competition. You can do everything right, and still not get the result you want.*

Finally, with respect to the Olympics and high performance, I've learned that:

Awareness is key to overcoming distractions. Many people aren't aware of the things that can distract them from their preparation.

So we spent a lot of time talking about the issues. We had data from other athletes who shared what caused their performance to be where it shouldn't have been, and the #1 constraint was distractions. Therefore, we were careful with how we handled our schedule, free time, and discipline in everything we did.

Performance Drives Confidence

A confident player is going to be a better player. I've realized that you can't have confidence without performance. My coaching approach is very performance-oriented.

If I can improve the athlete's performance, then I can improve the athlete's confidence.

There's nothing that I can sprinkle over them that says you're going to be a confident player.

- It's trusting the process
- It's trusting your preparation
- It's not making the game bigger than it really is

This game (softball) will never be life threatening. You can go 0-4 today; then I can walk you across the street to the Cancer Center where you'll find a bunch of little kids and you realize that you've actually had a really good day. Helping players keep the game in perspective is important.

We focus on helping our team control the controllables, which include your attitude, effort, and focus. At the end of the day, I want my players to look in the mirror and like what they see – that they are better people.

The reality is that there are not many kids that are going to make a living playing softball. Thus, my kids (players) are usually very good students.

I feel that my job here is to prepare my players for life after softball.

Hopefully, when they walk out of our Arizona softball program, they are better people. If you make them better people, then they are going to be more confident. The players understand how important it is to buy-in to the process – that the process is something you have to put at the top of the list on a day-to-day basis.

As a coach, your thank-you's come ten years after the players leave: *"Coach, thanks for kicking me in the butt. Today I know exactly what you're talking about because now I'm raising a family."* The lifelong lessons sometimes take a while. Truthfully, it's hard to go through a career as an athlete for four years and not walk away as a better person.

It's true that freshmen tend to walk into our program and get a little overwhelmed. The college-level game is completely different than what they've experienced in the past. So, I try to bring them back to their roots: *"Remember the first time you put on a uniform? You didn't have a worry in life."*

90% of what you worry about never happens.

You have total control over this game if you understand the process, preparation, and how to handle failure. In softball, you are playing a sport that is basically a game of failure. The best hitters get a hit three out of ten times. Seven out of ten times you're going to fail. My job is to teach you how to handle failure in a positive way.

In life, you're going to face the same curve balls. Life is not all roses and lollipops. It can be very challenging.

Great Leaders Create Adversity

My definition of failure is not controlling the controllables. That's the way I live my life. There are things I have control over and I'm going to control those things as well as I can. If I do that, then it's not a failure, but a setback that I can learn from. I think that's the biggest thing about failure:

What is it that I am learning from failure?

Remember Michael Jordan's quote, *"I've failed over and over and over again in my life and that's why I succeed."* Be reminded of Thomas Edison's trials when inventing the light bulb. Everyone has got to go through failure. I don't want our student-athletes to fear failure. That's one of my biggest things. You cannot have a fear of failure, not only to play this game, but to successfully live your life. I believe the only way you can do that is by controlling the things you have control over.

Now I do think we go through life fearing failure. I am sure that any athlete that puts on a uniform has a little fear of not doing well. But I don't think you can go through life fearing failure and be successful. You need to learn how to deal with failure.

You can prepare a team for adversity by creating adversity. I always tell our players that *"you have to learn how to feel comfortable being uncomfortable."* In athletics, we all understand that there's going to be times when you're uncomfortable. The challenge is to be able to conquer and overcome that discomfort. Once you do that, you realize that you can overcome it. But I don't think that you can ever put on a uniform and always be a winner.

Another vital key is being humble, respecting the game, and realize that things can happen. You have to be able to control what you can in victory and defeat – and draw lessons from both. For example, I've had some very good teams that didn't "win it." Then I had some teams that didn't think could win and won it!

There are so many intangibles in a team sport; intangibles such as chemistry, communication, and kids that really embrace pressure. One of the principles we teach is:

It's a gift to truly embrace pressure.

That's where we want you to be. We don't want you to fear pressure. We want you to embrace it.

Learning is the Master Key

Fear is real. That's one thing I've learned. I've also learned that I can control my fear. A lot of it is: What's your definition of fear? What exactly is it that you fear? What can happen?

The worst thing you will experience on a playing field is definitely not any worse than anything you'll have to go through in life. Listen, when you've lost a child (as I have), there's not much more that you're going to fear. The master key is learning how to handle the situation and do the best you can with it.

Some of my life lessons include:

- I've lost a child
- I've a lost a player
- I've lost a dad
- I've lost a wife

What else in life can be any tougher? My objective is to show our team that I have been able to rebound from adversity. No matter what happens to them, they can also rebound from adversity.

> *You set the example by choice. In coaching, the big thing is being real with kids. The more life lessons that I can share with our players, the better.*

I get very personal with my experiences to demonstrate that I'm a real person. Things happen – and you learn how to deal with it. You must have the "tools" and the "equipment" to overcome adversity. For me, my principles are very simple:

1. A strong family unit helps you deal with failure.
2. I have a strong passion for my profession. I've never worked a day in my life because I'm doing what I love to do. On the other hand, I can't be a slave to my profession and forget about my family.
3. My faith sustains me.

Life is More Than Winning Championships

Balance in life is very important. I want my athletes to understand what balance is. You don't want to put all of your eggs into softball. We want kids who are well-balanced, academically, athletically, and socially. If they become better people through achieving balance, then they will also become better players.

In the pursuit of excellence, there are times we find ourselves out of balance. I've been there and I share that story with our team. Back in 1994, I was coaching the U.S. national team in St. John's, Newfoundland. I had just won our 2nd championship here at Arizona and I was miserable – and

I couldn't figure it out. I was in St. John's for a month and a half in a little dorm room that felt like it was closing in on me. I came home from that trip, walked in my house, and my son (Michael) at the time was a sophomore in high school. He didn't say, "*Dad, welcome home, but Dad, we need to talk.*"

"*Dad, I want you to know that I love what you're doing. I love all these championships. I love you being a part of the national team. But I need you as a dad right now. Would you consider dropping out of the USA Coaching selection process so you can watch me play baseball?*"

That hit me like a ton of bricks and changed my life. I dropped out of the coaching pool and coached Michael for the next three summers. If it weren't for him…I was just sitting there losing the people I love the most and not even knowing it because I was pursuing excellence.

I thought my life revolved around winning championships.

This experience taught me a big, big lesson on balance. Once I got the balance, I became a better dad, a better coach, and a happier person. For me, that's what I attempt to teach young kids and coaches.

You measure balance by quality of time. Be present.

There were many times I'd be at the dinner table and mentally be a world away. Balance includes paying attention and small acts such as never missing a birthday, never missing a wedding, and calling my own children at least once a week to check in with them. It's the little things that make a huge difference.

Balance is not money. It's unconditional love, time, and caring. At the end of the day (and of my career), it's going to be all about the relationships I've built. No one is going to remember the year we won the championship. Truthfully, not that many people care. Ultimately, you have to think as an adult:

What is truly important to me?

For me, family is the key to everything and I try to run my teams as a big family.

You Can Become a Fearless Competitor

Susie Parra

Susie was a member of our Gold Medal USA Team and an influential leader in our first national championship. Before the championship game, Susie told our team, *"Let's go out and play to win, not to lose."*

As a freshman, she'd pitch five innings, then get in trouble in the sixth. I would put another pitcher in to relieve her. One year at regionals, I decided that she had to "grow up" so I left Susie out there on the mound when she things got rough. After that, I never had to take her out of a game again. Susie realized that: first, I had confidence in her. And second, she could get the job done. Susie was definitely the beginning of everything for us at Arizona.

Jennie Finch

Jennie was a kid who taught me a lot about balance. Jennie had total balance when she came to Arizona. She was great competitor and is a great person.

Lisa Fernandez

As far as a competitor, Lisa was one of the very best. The great thing about Lisa was that she reinvented herself every year. She had success for so many years. Lisa was always putting herself in the Olympic arena at every practice. She had that knack of being able to practice at a very high level. Lisa was very savvy for her age.

Leah O'Brien-Amico
I loved watching Leah play because she always had a smile on her face. Leah always looked like she loved playing the game. You couldn't tell if she was at practice or if she was at a gold medal game. She had the same look – that was a gift, and probably a trait that helped Leah handle pressure so successfully.

Crystl Bustos
Crystl was another fearless competitor. She could strike out on three pitches, come back to the dugout, lay her bat down, and say, *"I'm going to get her next time."* Crystl taught many young kids how to handle failure in a positive way.

I have been blessed to coach many great athletes. The greatest gift I've been given is being able to watch them grow as young ladies, seeing them have families, and interacting with their kids.

> *I used to think that I coached kids for four years and they leave, but that's not the case. I coach them for a lifetime.*

The players never "leave." That's the gift of the female athlete.

The 3 C's of Successful Coaching
I've always tried to be a real person, recognizing that I'm not sitting on a pedestal looking down on the players. I've been through the trials and tribulations that they may be going through. And I'm willing to share my

experiences. I've always tried to live my life by coaching through the 3 C's (and not because of my last name!):

1. **Competent.** I've always tried to be a student of the game. I try to find something new and different to reach a particular kid. I think that's the key.
2. **Consistent.** Good leaders are consistent. They are not up and down. You can rely on them every day. It's not going to change.
3. **Caring.** I care about our players as individuals. Part of that caring can be very vulnerable because sometimes you set yourself up for disappointment. We strive to build relationships based on trust, honesty, and respect.

> *Every time I make a life decision, I think about the 500+ athletes I've coached and the fact that I'd never want to disappoint them.*

To me, that can really make you vulnerable. Yet, that's the life I've chosen. That's the person that I am. Furthermore, I like who I am and I like what we represent. Whether we win or we don't win, the bottom line is that I've treated each athlete like my daughter. There's always a chance of being vulnerable, but that's part of being human.

Life is Precious
The loss of a child and a spouse has taught me how precious life is.

> *I encourage people to live each day like it's your last.*

I live my life that way because I know how quickly it can change. When I lost a child, I was twenty-four years old. We didn't have insurance at the time. I am literally seeing my life flash in front of me. It made me realize how important it was for me to be a provider.

As a result, I became a planner, from the financials to having back-up plans in place in every area of my life.

The loss of a child also brought me closer to my faith. You might as well wake up in the morning and choose to have a great day. It's up to you. It's allowed me to keep both life and the game in perspective. God does not play favorites.

When I lost Sue (my first wife) in 2004, it was right before the Olympic Games. I didn't know whether I was going to go (to the Olympics) or not. It was during this time that I found out how powerful family really was. I became acutely aware that I was playing a game that really isn't all that big. When Sue passed, the outpour from people all over the country and world made me realize how many people I have touched in one way or the other through the game of softball. I take that positive impact very seriously.

There's a power in what I do every day.

It's one of the reasons I always take the time to respond to as many emails and questions that I receive from people who want to learn more about the game.

The most important lesson I learned from all of this is the importance of balance. When Sue passed away, I didn't even know the color of our checkbook. I didn't even know what my kids needed because all I did each day was get up and go to work. I'd go back home and everything was taken care of. I received a real snapshot of life and what's truly important in life. I also became a better father to my kids because I had to. I now had to take care of the daily things that they needed.

Sometimes we (staff, players, and colleagues...) talk about the profession and how it can affect things.

*I know too many people that are so driven. I wish I could
give everyone a national championship to show them
that it's not going to change your life.*

Before this stuff happened, I was very bad at saying no to people. I was trying to do everything I could possibly do for our country and our sport. Now, my very first thing is, *"First and foremost, I better take care of myself."*

Sue was perfectly healthy one moment. The next she had a brain aneurysm. The second thing I do is pay attention to what's really important to me. I'm still very driven to do my job, but my job is not going to take over my life.

I've been blessed to have very good people around me, like my mom, our local monsignor, and many, many others. For that, I'm always grateful.

8 Wildcat Leadership Lessons from Mike Candrea

1. Share your stories of trials to help other people.
2. Achieve balance in your life.
3. Define success for yourself.
4. Emphasize the process over the result.
5. Focus on what you can control.
6. Be passionate about what you do.
7. Remain open to the possibilities.
8. Master the 3 C's: Be competent, consistent, and caring.

LEADERSHIP CONVERSATION WITH TARA VANDERVEER

MOST WINS IN WOMEN'S COLLEGE BASKETBALL HISTORY

Provided by CoachVidal.com

Tara VanDerveer is the head women's basketball coach at Stanford University, where she led the Cardinal to two NCAA Women's Division 1 Basketball Championships in 1990 and 1992. 4x National Coach of the Year, VanDerVeer served as USA head coach at the 1996 Olympic Games. Van Derveer was inducted into the Women's Basketball Hall of Fame in 2002. On December 16, 2020 she passed Pat Summit for most wins in women's college basketball history. (The following content represents Coach VanDerveer's own words.)

Be Yourself

My parents were both teachers. Our family was kind of a team. I'm the oldest of five. Both my parents really managed our family like a team. They worked well together to set really good examples and were great mentors for me and my brothers and sisters.

They had constant little sayings and messages. One of my mom's favorites was, **"Be like a duck. Don't let things bother you. Let them roll off your back."** This helped me learn how to deal with adversity. Another popular message was, "Be yourself." My father was very much the same. A few of his ideas were

- **"Leave something better than you found it."**
- **"Repetition of errors shows a lack of intelligence."**

My mom always encouraged me to be positive. If I got into it with my brothers and sisters, I'd have to come in and regroup. There was a lot of coaching going on all the time.

Life is Too Short to Have a Bad Day

In a nutshell, my coaching philosophy and success habits can be summed up as follows:

1. Have a great day every day.
2. Be enthusiastic about what you do.
3. Outwork people through your dedication and great effort.
4. Enjoy what you're doing.
5. Have a positive attitude.
6. Take care of yourself. I make sure I get my rest, eat right, and work out.
7. Be a good example for your team and your staff.
8. Surround yourself with really good people of integrity.
9. Set high standards for yourself and the people that you work with. Be very demanding.

It always comes back to the people that you're around—their honesty, commitment, genuineness, and integrity. Life is too short to be dealing with a lot of drama, bad chemistry, negativity, and problems. Here at Stanford, we promote a positive work environment.

How to Deal With Change

As you get older, you want to do things better. Situations change. Our world is different now than thirty-to-forty years ago when I started coaching. The experiences that our players have are different. I didn't have email, cell phones, and social media.

Coaching in today's world is certainly challenging. Parents are a lot more in your face. There's a lot more negativity and entitlement. Historically, parents have always thought their kids should play or get the ball more. Today, they just seem to express it more. You can also be anonymous while expressing your feelings. You can post things that go viral.

In collegiate sports, your athletic director is key. It's vitally important to have good communication with your administration, because I have had administrators who were not supportive and it's hell. If you're trying to battle parents, entitled players, fan negativity, and a weak administrator, you're in trouble. That's not a pretty sight.

Overall, I've been fortunate to have great administrators, great parents, and some really mature players. For example, one time a parent may have over-stepped their bounds, and the player wanted to meet with me the next day. I was ready. The player said to me:

**"I play for you. Tell me what you want me
to do. I respect your decisions."**

Honestly, it was mind-blowing.

Another story: We had a player on the Olympic team who had a parent who kept saying, "You should be playing more." And the player told the parent, "Stop. I'm going to get the same gold medal as the other players on this team, and that's what's important to me— WINNING A GOLD MEDAL." That kind of support for your team is rare. I tell stories like these to members of our Stanford team to help them deal with that kind of stuff with their own parents.

Maximize Your Potential

I communicate with our team that every day is a challenge to work hard, be positive, and improve. As a coach, my goal is to help each player reach her potential and be the best player she can be. Of course there are days when it's a battle if you have players who are not motivated or coachable. Although I'm competitive enough that even if that happens, I'm not going to give in. I'm going to work doubly hard to do a better job.

At Stanford, it's a very different place to work. At my former employers such as Ohio State or Idaho, if players are really unhappy with their playing times, they'll just transfer. At Stanford, the players love the university and culture too much to leave. They'll stick it out. However, some players, while totally loving the school, still may not bring their best selves to the gym. Listen, it's hard to walk away from $75,000 a year scholarship.

Build a Competitive Culture

Culture is interesting and you are constantly figuring things, particularly within the NCAA rules. As a team committed to building strong bonds, we've done rope courses or had different people come in, such as national championship coaches, to speak with our team. We've had former players like John Elway—winners who can share what competing means and what it's like to compete at the highest level. Former Olympians have visited with our program. We've been extremely fortunate in this regard.

I think a championship culture starts with your staff

- Being positive,
- Being encouraging, and
- Being enthusiastic.

It's a challenge. For example, right now (September 2015), we're at the very beginning of the year on campus and our staff is heavily recruiting. So it's a balancing act. It's hard to juggle all the things you need to be doing, but what I to do individually with each player is go to the dorm rooms, see them in their environment, talk to them about how they're doing in class, about their lives and families—just to get to know them. You recruit players and spend a lot of time with them, but getting to truly know them is key.

I also show the players a little bit of what my relationship is with former players. There's a spectrum of opportunity. For example, some players leave Stanford and I might not ever hear from them again. Whereas other players, I'll talk to them, text with them; it's a wide scope of how the relationship can be. The players decide.

- **What relationship do you want to have with your coaches?**
- **Do you understand what my role is as your coach?**

I always make sure our players have my cell phone number, and I have theirs. My office is open. I'm available at any time. We have kids from all over the country; and are a little bit like "parents-in-residence."

Don't Take No for an Answer

The very best teams have players that love to play. They love the game of basketball. Practice is something great athletes look forward to. Championship teams have players who always want to get better. Players who are

- Excited about games
- Unselfish
- Committed to getting along with each other
- Focused on winning collectively over individual accomplishments

- Hard working
- Talented

Attitude and effort are two huge keys to championship teams. Those are the teams that I think that are really motivated and competitive. **Championship teams don't take no for an answer.** They are going to win, period. Don't get in their way!

What's Your Game Plan?

John Wooden used to say, **"I can beat you with my team, and I can beat you with your team."** Coaches have a formula and the better ones have some things figured out more than other coaches.

There are certain formulas that fit your own personality and how you teach and coach. For example, you can give the same ingredients to five different chefs, and only one of them will make an amazing meal out of those same ingredients. Whereas, if you give those same ingredients to me and I wouldn't even know what to do with them. I wouldn't know how to combine those things.

Personally, I grew up watching a lot of basketball. I like the 10,000 hour principle in Malcolm Gladwell's book, *Outliers*. I watched and watched and watched and studied basketball. When I put coaching approach together, I think my strengths lean more toward X's and O's than touchy-feely. For me, the technical side of basketball—analyzing video and showing players what they need to be doing is my superpower.

Of course there are some players who simply want to hear how great they are and be encouraged to keep shooting the ball. As leaders, coaches, and teachers, we communicate to our team:

This is what we need to do.
This is how we can beat this other team.
This is our game plan.

For the most part, our Stanford teams have overachieved. And when our teams have underachieved, it's been due to injuries, immaturity (we're limited in who we can recruit), and there's no changing horses in the middle by bringing in a junior college player. **There's nobody coming in on a white horse to save the team.** At Stanford, it's 'this is who's here because this is who can get in academically.'

Sometimes, we simply may not have the leadership that we need, nor the skill set, nor the depth—each or all of which can make for a hard year.

Now, when we beat teams that have more talent (e.g., five all-stars), a lot of it is that the other team isn't as cohesive as our team. Those teams may not have a structured game plan, whereas our kids know the game plan and will follow-through on the game plan. A lot of people will say, "You have all these smart kids." Well, book smart and basketball smart is not always the same thing.

We are very clear: **This is our game plan.** We need our players to buy-in to our game plan and for the most part they do.

Know Who You Are

Teaching the fundamentals is really important as well as having a team identity. I ask our team

- **What is our team identity?**
- **What do we hang our hat on?**

For example, this year's (2015-16) team, I think our best chance to be successful is to be up-tempo, which means that we have to run and be excited about running. This is how we're going to play—by pushing the tempo. We'll work hard to force turnovers defensively and rebound so that we can run. Other teams may be like, "We have five players. We'll walk the ball up the court and go inside to our big post player." Another team may be like, "Our pick and roll is the best play."

As a coach, one of my roles is to figure out which is the best identity and make sure people understand it and buy into it.

Expect to Win

To keep success going, it's important to come back to the head coach and the program. You have a legacy. For example, look at Dick Gould (former men's tennis coach at Stanford) and seventeen NCAA national team championships. Gould's success was not an accident. It didn't just happen.

Stanford's Dick Gould knows something that other people don't know. Gould is doing something that other people are not doing. He's got it figured out in a way that other people don't have it figured out.

Our success on the basketball court is not that extreme in a positive sense, yet I do believe we have things figured out on the keys of what gives us the best chance to be successful. We develop a game plan and communicate that game plan to our players. We drill our players and tailor our strategies based on the personnel we have.

**Our goal is to maximize our players' strengths
and minimize our players' weaknesses.**

When you play at Stanford, you develop a mentality that you *expect to win*. One of my favorite coaches is Brooks Johnson, the former track and field coach here at Stanford. Brooks was our 1984 Olympics track coach and his philosophy was

Winners find a way to win.

Brooks developed that mentality in his programs. The mindset that "we're about business and we're going to outwork people. Our team—the people in this room, are going to be more committed, more cohesive, and do what it takes to be champions."

Player Development

We look at a person's statistics. For example, let's take a point guard. You want to have a 3:1 assist-to-turnover ratio or you want to shoot at least a certain number of free throws to show that you're attacking the basket. We look at development from the standpoint that this is an ideal point guard. We'll then meet with our point guard(s) and tap into our huge video closet. We use video a lot to show players: that this is *how* we want to expand your game. As a point guard, you're attacking the basket, pushing the ball in transition, and defending in certain ways. And our coaching staff takes this approach with every position on the team.

We also give the players very specific feedback after every game.

"Here are three things you did well. Here are two things we want to improve."

We intentionally use drills in practice to teach details and reinforce fundamentals such as how you warm up, where and how you stand (when you hear the national anthem), what you can expect, how you get your towel when you come out of the game, and where you sit on the bench. There are no surprises.

Jennifer Azzi came in to Stanford and made herself an All-American. She lived in Tennessee and the University of Tennessee didn't recruit her. She lived twenty miles from the Vols campus. Yet, Jennifer came to Stanford, became a two-time All-American, an Olympian (1996), and led her team to a national championship. Jennifer became a fabulous player.

Nneka Ogwumike came in to Stanford and honestly I had a coach say to me. "She's not as good as I thought she was going to be." Nneka was not player of the year as a freshman, but she was the number one player in the country as a senior, and the #1 draft pick in the 2012 WNBA.

Katie Starburg came in to Stanford and people looked at her and said, "She has a funky shot." We had four freshman at the time. Each of my assistants chose another player to work with. So I worked with Katie and she became the leading scorer here at Stanford. When we started working together, Katie said to me, "I know you probably want to change my shot." I replied, "No, not if it goes in." I was like if you can score, "you go girl." Katie became the 1997 Naismith Player of the Year.

Candice Wiggins came in to Stanford and became our one 4-time All American. I don't know if she would've achieved such heights if she would have gone to other places. It's important to understand: It's not just the coaches. It's the upperclassmen on the team, who welcomed her in as a freshman. They encouraged her. They mentored her. And they shared in her joy of being a great player. They were never jealous of her. They were proud that Candice became an All-American. Today (as of 2015), Candice plays guard for the New York Liberty of the Women's National Basketball Association (WNBA).

Keep Raising the Bar

When I was the head coach at Ohio State, we had a great, great team. Then the Stanford job opened up. When I shared with my dad (a Dartmouth graduate) that I was looking at Stanford (in reality I had already accepted the job), he said, **"Don't take that job. You'll never win."** So I told him, "I took it." We got off the phone and my dad said to my mom, "Tara will be unemployed, coming home, and living with us in three months." But I refused to go back to cold upstate New York.

At Stanford, we have to recruit the best of the brightest, period. Now, there may be some other baggage that comes with it. As a staff, we'll go watch an impressive player and I'll ask one of my assistants what her name is, and she'll say, "two-point, you don't need to know," as in 2.0 GPA—not getting in Stanford. For us, it's all about who can get in academically.

If the player can get in, we do our best to make it work. There have been some times where I've had to say to a player, "You're a great player, an All-American, but you're disruptive to our team and you need to go somewhere else. Or I'll give you the scholarship but you will not play on the team." And believe it or not, we won a national championship the next year with that same player, and she did not play on the team.

We don't have a specific character profile. If the student-athlete can get academically admitted to Stanford and are talented enough to help us, we'll do our best to make it work. Our recruiting pool is very small. We obviously have more good than bad, but there are some absolute bad apples out there.

We recruit all over the country as well as internationally. Recruiting is "different places for different people." For example, Stanford is a really unique challenge. We are the only school that is consistently ranked top five academically and in women's basketball. If someone is truly motivated academically and athletically, Stanford is a great fit for a Jayne Appel, Nneka Ogwumike, Candice Wiggins, or Sonja Henning. But it's hard to find those players.

Once your team gets really good, the bar goes even higher.

Winning the Gold

I started coaching the Olympic women's basketball team on October 1st, 1995. We were together for nine months to win the gold medal in Atlanta. It was the most amazing group because we were so focused every day. The team worked so hard. There was not a bad day. We had numerous trips, travelled all over the world. We experienced bad food, bad flights, and a particularly frightening airplane ride over Australia.

85

If you were to write a book about teams or do a movie, this was a team that you dream about coaching. It was why you would coach. As a coaching staff, we had to drag these players off the court—they enjoyed practice so much. They'd want to play one-on-one, keep shooting, and there were never any issues with people getting along.

"This Woman Is Crazy!"

The Olympic team bonded not-so-much against me but in a way that said, *"This woman is crazy."* Each of them were used to being the best player. At the time for example, Sheryl Swoopes could only bench press forty pounds, yet we were lifting three times a week regardless of our schedule. They were like, "Coach is crazy."

Actually, I just saw a bunch of them when Lisa Leslie was inducted into the Hall of Fame. Of course, the Olympic team loves to tell stories at my expense. They said did you pay off the referees in Russia to make it so hard because they were always getting called for "three seconds." Seeing these players twenty years later, what they remember is that it was tough—and awesome.

Interestingly enough, I didn't select the team. The players were already picked. So I went in with a bit of a chip on my shoulder because I felt we needed one extra tall girl, a post player that wasn't selected. The first thing I did was give them a summer conditioning program that I graded. For example, if a player was supposed run 3 miles and only ran two, she'd receive a red check.

**One of our main themes was that
we were going to outwork
the rest of the world.**

At the time, Americans were viewed as lazy and sloppy. I said, *"We are going to outwork everyone else."* We had yet to win a world championship, and we had not won a gold medal in the last Olympics. There was a certain attitude: us against the world plus the fact that we were hosting the Olympics.

The first thing we did was a two mile test/training run in altitude with 40mph winds and forty-degree weather, and one of the players, Dawn Staley says, "We're not going to run today are we?" I said, "Yes, we are because this is when I learn the most about people." And the team was like, "THIS WOMAN IS CRAZY!"

I was very demanding. These were players that were used to being the prima donnas on their team. In international basketball, you must "run back" and help your teammates. So Lisa Leslie, our center, doesn't hustle back on a play—I immediately have a substitute at the table ready to go in for her. The players would never admit it, but they were used to being coddled. My attitude was "no," this is all about taking home the gold.

It's about winning a gold medal. It's not about me being your best friend.

If a player didn't do the workouts right, we had a "Breakfast Club." The players were not used to that. There were only three players who weren't in the Breakfast Club. And you had to work yourself out of the Club. The players laugh about it now and are like, "*I don't wanna have to be in that Breakfast Club.*"

We never scouted the teams to get ready to compete. I didn't want to give the players that advantage. We did things to make the environment harder, like lifting three times a week. We would arrive in a city, and the first thing we would do is work out. They were exhausted, but it's scientifically proven that if you work out immediately upon arrival, it helps you adjust to the time change. Again, they were like, "*This woman is crazy!*"

The pundits asked, "How are you going to handle the professionals as a college coach?" and I replied

"The amateurs are the ones that I will have trouble with."

My leadership approach is similar at Stanford. You come in and get it done. I am very respectful of our kids' time. We are very organized. We get to work and move on.

Hire the Right People

I've made some bad hiring mistakes and I've learned from them. For the most part I will hire people that I know or people that are highly recommended. I interview candidates and really attempt to get to know them. I talk to references, trying to do as much due diligence as I possibly can. I look for a fit with them and with our program. Yet, there have been times when I've hired some people and it's been a disaster because...

- They weren't loyal
- They didn't have the work ethic
- They lacked high intelligence ('If players can trip you up, you're in trouble')
- They lacked teaching skills

For the most part however, I feel really good about our staffing history. I'd give myself an "A" grade on eight out of ten hires. On the remaining two, I have some "C" grades, and in those cases, you have to make changes.

Most of my assistants have a vision to become a head coach, but it's not a requirement. The key is that they must share my vision for our team. They don't have to agree with me in the office—my ideas get shot down all the time. But when we're in front of the team, we have to be on the same page.

I don't want to be the only brain in the room. I want to win. I ask for people's ideas, from coaches to players. We don't have to do things my way. I'm not a genius. I want to win. Here's the question,

"Are you truly finding the right person who is a great fit for your program?"

There are different people at different times. I've hired people that have been fired. Stanford, to a certain extent, has been what I call "The Recycling Bin." I've hired a lot of people to help them get back on their feet. Especially in women's basketball and women's sports in general, coaches are not given a second chance; whereas guys are recycled all the time.

Prepare for Success

I've been fortunate to be around people who love the sport of basketball and have a passion for athletics. There are a lot of people that are part of the Stanford Women's Basketball tree.

For example, Sonja Henning at Nike. Yet, it wasn't like a light bulb went off for her while she was on campus. In fact, Sonja's junior high school coach understood that she was a very bright young lady, super talented, and encouraged her academically.

Sonja later joined us, and from Stanford she absolutely blossomed. She's brilliant to begin with, hard working, and was a great player. While at Stanford, Sonja networked really well, then went to law school at Duke. She was just prepared for success. Being here at Stanford, Sonja played with Jennifer Azzi, Katy Steding, and other Olympians. Sonja was also around other male players at the time such as baseball player Mike Mussina and basketball player Todd Lichte.

I can't take any credit for Sonja's success. She was extremely motivated. For example, one time after practice, I was running one way, she was running the other way—we never said a word to each other, but the message to me was *"You've got to pick up the practices."*

Indiana Coaching Legend Bobby Knight

I loved watching basketball practice at Indiana. I actually attended every men's basketball practice for three consecutive years. If I was there, I was in the gym watching.

It was very clear that Bobby Knight had a formula.

- You're going to play physical
- You're going to play team basketball
- You're going to move, screen, and play defense

Bobby Knight was a great teacher. He was not a screamer like many people might think. The play would happen. He would walk down the court and say, "Quinn Buckner, I need you to do this." If Quinn or any other player didn't do what he asked, they would hear about it.

Coach Knight was very clear on how you play basketball at Indiana.

I think that example is something that wasn't wasted on me.

6 Cardinal Leadership Lessons from Tara VanDerveer

1. Approach each day with enthusiasm unknown to mankind (Jim Harbaugh).
2. Be enthusiastic and excited about what you do.
3. Care about your teammates and other people.
4. Challenge yourself to be the best person that you can be.
5. Look in the mirror. "Your mirror is your judge." *Are you becoming the best you can possibly be, personally and professionally?*
6. Be genuine. Don't do things for the wrong reason.

At the end of the day, I like the nitty-gritty, the everyday of being in the gym. Honestly, the praise and accolades are wasted on me.

I like the journey.

LEADERSHIP RESEARCH ACKNOWLEDGMENTS

For their friendship, inspiration, support, and insight over the years, René and Steve would like to thank the following leaders:

Dr. Jim Afremow, Doug Archibald, Marcos Asse, Bobby Bayliss, Dr. Ann Beatty, Jeff Bell, Jay Berger, David Berndt, Ronni Bernstein, Gayle Birdsong, Brian Boland, Andy Bollwerk, Mark Bowser, Andy Brandi, Frank Brennan, Les Butler, Preston Cameron, Mike Candrea, Tom Carnahan, Tim Cass, Dave Charest, Terryl Curry, Brad Dancer, Frank Danzo, Sarah Dubberke, Derek Dunwiddie, Ian Duvenhage, Mike Edles, Mark Edwards, Roger Follmer, Suzanne Fontaine, Allen Fox, Rodney Harmon, Roel Harryvan, Bryan Heathman, Eric Hernandez, Shep Hyken, Ken Goldberg, Dan Goldie, Paul Goldstein, Jon Gordon, Dick Gould, Teri Griege, Rose Hanley, Tim Helm, Mike Hogan, Eric Humes, Dan Isom, Helen Jardine, Glen Justis, Rusty Keeley, Chuck Kinyon, Pat Knoerle-Jordan, Paul Lacroix, Dena Ladd, Suzanne Langlois, Steve Lipic, Dr. Jim Loehr, Angel Lopez, Alaina Macia, Rick Macci, GeGe Mix, Pat Murphy, Tony Naughton, Mark Neal, Ben Newman, Kara Newmark, Lisa Nichols, Lisette Ortega-Vidal, Greg Patton, Laurie Phillips, Kelly Pollock, Bob Putnam, John O'Neil, Gayle Randa, Alan Robbins, Dr. Paul Roetert, Lynne Rolley, Jeff Salzenstein, Nick Saviano, Ray Scott, Dr. Jason Selk, Harold Solomon, Harlan Steinbaum, Brad Stine, Lisa Stone, David Straub, Scott Thielke, Robin Tucker, Tara Van der Veer, Rich Vanderwal, Bill Wallace, Paul Wardlaw, John Whitlinger, Chris Widener, Barry Worth.

ABOUT THE AUTHORS

 **René Vidal** is the head coach of men's and women's tennis at McKendree University. A six-time NCAA Championship Coach at Boise State, Colgate, and Mississippi State, he was voted Patriot League Women's Coach of the Year and is highly regarded as one of *America's top coaches.* Coach Vidal is the author of 4 books and a nation-ally recognized speaker for his seminar, *"Winning Leadership: 9 Principles for Building Champions."* To book Coach Vidal for your next corporate or association event, email rene@renevidal.com or visit www.renevidal.com.

 **STEVE FINKELSTEIN** is an accomplished business coach, author, facilitator, and speaker. He is the cofounder of Experience on Demand, which was voted the number-one best consulting firm in St. Louis by *Small Business Monthly* (2013, 2014, 2016, and 2017). In 2016, the organization was a BBB Torch Award winner. An expert in strategic planning and business execution, Steve helps clients achieve their business objectives by developing a culture of innovation, collaboration, planning, and execution. A former partner at Deloitte and Grant Thornton, Steve is coauthor of *Play Smart to Win in Business.* In 2016 Steve received the University of Missouri Distinguished Career Achievement Award, and in 2017 he was selected as one of the "100 St. Louisans You Should Know to Succeed in Business." To learn more, visit www.experience-on-demand.com.